I WAS ALWAYS ENOUGH

ANTONIA B. JOHNSON

I WAS ALWAYS ENOUGH
@Copyright 2020 by ANTONIA B. JOHNSON
All rights reserved. No part of this book maybe reproduced or transmitted in any form or by any means without written permission from the author.
ISBN: 978-1-953638-00-7
Printed in the United States of America

This book or parts there of may not be reproduced in any form, stored in a retrieval system, or transmitted in any form by any means-electronic, mechanical, photocopy, recording, or otherwise-without prior written permission of the publisher, except as provided by United States of America copyright law.

PUBLISHER
TA MEDIA & PRODUCTIONS LLC
DALLAS, TX 75240
www.PUBLISHYOURBOOKTODAY.INFO
WWW.TAMEDIACO.COM

Unless otherwise noted, all Scripture quotations are taken from the Holy Bible, King James Version
(PUBLIC DOMAIN PER BIBLEGATEWAY.COM)
Holy Bible, New International Version®, NIV® Copyright ©1973, 1978, 1984, 2011 by Biblica, Inc.® Used by permission. All rights reserved worldwide.
The Holy Bible, English Standard Version. ESV® Text Edition: 2016. Copyright © 2001 by Crossway Bibles, a publishing ministry of Good News Publishers.

DEDICATION

MY VERY FIRST BOOK!!! is dedicated to all of the women in my life, especially my mom (Pearl), my bonus moms (Delonda and Rosa), my sisters (Kenishe and Lakeisha), my daughter (Cailyn), and my niece (Nyah). It is dedicated to all of the women in my family and the women who I am blessed to call friends. It is dedicated to every woman who has ever felt unworthy, unloved, rejected, and abandoned, who as a result, chose the wrong relationships because of her desire to love and be loved in return. Sometimes we just get it wrong, and that is okay. Now it is time to get it right. You owe it to yourself to love from a healed place.

INTRODUCTION

Imagine going through life thinking that you have got a handle on everything that comes your way, and then BOOM, reality hits you in the face. You look up and you do not know where you are or how you got there. You have just been getting by and not taking inventory on what you have or what you have lost, which is essentially yourself. You realize that you do not know what it means to love yourself and that you gave all you had, even without reciprocity. You are mentally and spiritually bankrupt.

I WAS ALWAYS ENOUGH walks you through real life experiences where lessons were learned as a result of making unwise decisions. Those decisions were made from a place where there was a lack of self-love, there were feelings of rejection, as well as not understanding the meaning of worth. Each chapter title is a principle of what I have learned throughout the years. You will see the ups, the downs, and the triumphs that arose from trauma. You will see how focusing on God can help turn life around and set you on an entirely different path. You will see that He will give you beauty for ashes (Isaiah 61:3).

Here is an encouragement to you, my reader: No one determines your worthiness. You were always enough!

ABOUT THE AUTHOR

Antonia B. Johnson is a Chicago native and mother of 3 beautiful purposes: Cornelius (Lance), Colyn, and Cailyn. She is an author, speaker, and lover of people. As founder of the A Babe Renewed Project (girls mentoring), she facilitates empowerment workshops for teenage girls and women. She always shows up as a positive influence in conversation as well as on social media, and believes that when given the chance, always allow your light to shine brightly. She serves at her local church, All Nations Worship Assembly. Antonia is an overcomer and uses the lessons and wisdom gained through her experiences to help guide others on their journey to overcoming.

IT WAS ME...

the quiet girl who didn't tell my friends that I was lying on my back with the same men who said they only wanted sex, the same men who claimed they broke up with their girls and conveniently disappeared after they got what they wanted from me, and the same men that I didn't require a relationship from because I didn't know my worth. Yeah, that was me. But I wanted to feel needed.

He told me, "I can't lie, I just want to see what it's like." And I gave it to him. After the fact, we both wanted more (sex), but he remained clear that it was just sex...and I kept going.

He told me, "we're not together. We just broke up." But I gave it to him. After the fact, he pulled a disappearing act. He was with her. He came back and I fussed...but I kept going.

He told me, "let's just go with the flow and see where it leads." And I still gave it to him. After the fact, he said that he didn't want me to change because of a title, so let's just continue to do what we have been doing...still, I kept going.

IT WAS ME...

who desired big breasts, a thin waist, and a big butt (36", 24", 36"). Besides, that's what all the guys liked, right? I wanted to be told I was sexy too! That's what I saw in the videos and in the clubs. Yeah, that was me. I was looking for validation.

He told me, "you don't have to hide your body. It looks amazing. Your breasts are just the right size, turn around, girl you thick!" He blew my head up...and I gave it to him. After the fact, he was addicted to me. For me, it was okay at best...I kept going.

IT WAS ME...

who chose bad relationship after bad relationship never thinking to heal first. I was looking to fill a void. I just wanted to be accepted.

He said he wanted to date and work toward a relationship with me. We spent a lot of time together and had some amazing moments. The chemistry was off the chain. We would laugh and have hour long conversations. I gave it to him. After the fact, I asked him if we were still working toward a relationship, but he said he wanted to date other women (including sex) and still have me; that he would still tell the other women about me. I told him that I was not accepting that. He eventually apologized for not being honest upfront. I kept moving.

I became sick and tired of being sick and tired. I started to learn that I was worth so much more than what I was accepting. I deserved more than what I kept settling for in those situationships.

IT WAS ME...

who needed freedom! I needed God now more than ever before! I needed to know who I was. I needed to know my worth. I needed to know that I was enough. God showed me that.

It was me who gained a new level of wisdom and understanding from everything that I had experienced. I partnered with God, and He took me on a journey of healing that would change the trajectory of my life!

IT WAS GOD…

who told me not to waste my pain by sharing what I have learned, and not to be ashamed of my story. I am free!

TABLE OF CONTENTS

I AM WORTH IT! I KNOW WHO I AM! I AM ENOUGH! 2

I LOVE MYSELF SO MUCH MORE! 11

I AM NOT AFRAID TO SAY NO! 18

I AM MUCH HAPPIER BECAUSE I REALIZED THAT A RELATIONSHIP DID NOT COMPLETE OR FULFILL ME! 31

I AM ASKING THE IMPORTANT QUESTIONS IN THE BEGINNING! 35

WHEN SOMEONE SHOWS YOU WHO THEY ARE, BELIEVE THEM! 40

IF I WANT SOMETHING SERIOUS, I CANNOT SETTLE FOR "THIS" UNTIL "THAT" COMES ALONG 46

HEALING IS IMPORTANT...FOR YOU AND FOR THEM. 51

LISTEN TO WHAT HE SAYS (AND DOES NOT SAY), BUT OBSERVE WHAT HE DOES! 55

IF YOU BELIEVE IN GOD, AND YOU HEAR FROM HIM, DO NOT SECOND GUESS IT! 59

THERAPEUTIC HELP DOES NOT MAKE YOU CRAZY, IT HELPS YOU GAIN CLARITY 62

ANGER IS A DETERRENT TO HEALTHY COMMUNICATION! 66

THEY CANNOT LOVE YOU CORRECTLY IF THEY DO NOT LOVE THEMSELVES 70

BUILD PURPOSEFUL RELATIONSHIPS! .. 74

DIVORCE PAST RELATIONSHIPS THAT ARE IN YOUR HEAD! 78

I AM WORTH IT! I KNOW WHO I AM! I AM ENOUGH!

1

For you created my inmost being; you knit me together in my mother's womb. I praise you because I am fearfully and wonderfully made; your works are wonderful; I know that full well. My frame was not hidden from you when I was made in the secret place, when I was woven together in the depths of the earth. Your eyes saw my unformed body; all the days ordained for me were written in your book before one of them came to be. (Psalm 139:13-16 NIV)

In recent years, this is the scripture that made me realize that I was always enough. I have read it many times before, but it became apparent as I was praying asking God to show me who I was. I was enough even before I was a thought. God knew that I would be here, and he anticipated my arrival. He knew everything that I would experience, everything that I would succeed, everything that I would fail, and everything that I would overcome. And the way that God was so mindful of someone like me, makes me have a deep love for Him like no other.

Throughout my young adult years, you could not tell me that I did not know my worth, that I did not know who I was, or that I was not enough. My head was so high in the clouds, that I just knew I was "all that and a bag of chips." My perception of who I thought I was, was my own fallacy. It had nothing to do with being a woman who knew her worth or her "black girl magic" superpower. Unfortunately, it had everything to do with the men that I was attracting and choosing, sex, and the naivety in feeling as if I could do anything that I had pleased without having to suffer the consequences.

Back then, I had no clue about who I was or who I was supposed to be. I was a girl with rejection issues. My rejection issues stemmed from people making fun of my skin complexion and my "nappy" (natural) hair, being rejected by boys, picked on by girls, family, and the yearning for love from my father in what I considered the most critical years of my life.

I grew up thinking that my siblings' father was my father (I still affectionately call him my pops). Although I was only 5 years old, I remember as clear as day when he sat me down on his lap and told me that he was not my father, and that I was going to meet my biological dad. I cried because to me, he was my daddy. I did not understand it at that time.

When I saw my dad, I remember him and his wife giving me a Strawberry Shortcake doll and a few other presents, but the doll is the only thing I could remember. I treasured her and I loved my daddy. When they departed, he put his number on a piece of paper and told me to make sure I called him sometimes. I did.

My beautiful mother raised my siblings and me, and we moved around a lot. There were no cell phones; so, when we abruptly moved from Cabrini Green on the near north side (Chicago) to Gary, Indiana, all contact was lost. That piece of paper that was in my room with my dad's number on it, gone. My mom did not have his number. I was beyond devastated. I was 7 when we moved. We moved quite a few times after that. Before I even knew who God was, I remember looking out of the window and praying that my dad would just come and save the day. I was 13 when we reunited.

By that time, my feelings of validation and acceptance came from the boys who paid attention to me. The attention gave me a false sense of high self-esteem, and as a result, the rejection that I was dealing with opened up the door to lust.

I lost my virginity at 14. Before that, there was a boy in 8th grade that I allowed to touch me in ways that he should not have. He was also the first boy that I ever thought loved me, and I thought I loved him too. Unfortunately, that is when my curiosity for sex began. I had no idea that any kind of sexual act would stir up something on the inside of me that would be hard to break for years to come. Subsequently, I started to attract men who only wanted to be physical. Although I wanted more than that, I started making unwise decisions and finding myself in situationships. I wish I had known sooner in life that I was worth the wait.

Today, being worth it means knowing my value, my true value -without discount, not thrifted, and not for sale. I am a woman delivered from the spirit of rejection and even lust. Perfect? Nah. Delivered? Yes! It does not bother me if someone sees me and does not "see" me. I know who I am! The way I see myself has not only been shaped by the mistakes I made, but ultimately my being molded by God, and shifting my mind to believe what His word says. I had to learn to speak what God spoke and believe it in my heart. I am the apple of God's eye, that He will not lose sight of me (Psalm 17:8 KJV).

What God saw was good. I am everything He created me to be, as Jill Scott says, "from my hair follicles to my toenails." He even knew that I would make unwise decisions, and He still thought of me as wonderful. Although my mind had changed a few times about God, He has never changed His mind about me. He will never change. Jesus Christ is the same yesterday, today, and forever (Hebrews 13:8 KJV).

Seeing myself the way that God saw me took separation. Separation from past ideals, separation from certain people, separation from a life I thought I wanted, to God literally showing me how He saw me and what He desired of me. He loved me when I thought no one else loved me. He thought of me when people forgot about me and I forgot about myself. He rescued me when I was at a point of no return. He comforted me. He was my Jehovah Rapha -my healer. I have been going through a process of healing my entire life, and He has been right there. Now I know what it feels like to lay beside still waters because I have been through plenty of tsunamis.

I am enough! I have enough! I WAS ALWAYS ENOUGH! God made me with just enough pizzazz, enough intelligence, enough wit, enough sense of humor, enough grit, enough glory, enough faith, enough to be all that He has called me to be. Forgive me, my mind went directly to Meghan the Stallion's, I'm a Savage...classy, bougie, ratchet--never mind. I digress. I know you sang it though. But seriously, the ingredients that God concocted to make me were good and simply enough. What I need is already within me and I just had to grow and develop in that.

I LOVE MYSELF SO MUCH MORE!

2

To love yourself involves more than just saying it. What are you doing to show yourself love? What kind of decisions are you making that say, I love who I am?

For a long time, I settled. I settled for friendships, for second fiddle, not putting myself first, and for relationships. I wanted people to stay in my life. I loved hard. Wait, I tried to love others harder than I loved myself. I did not realize that the price of loving should not cost losing myself. Read that again.

I did not like to lose people because it always made me revert back to feeling rejected. It also made me feel unloved, so I fought for my relationships; even when they were not God's best for me. Matter of fact, I had no idea of what God's best was. All I knew was that when people stayed, it probably meant they loved me. But some people stayed because I allowed myself to be convenient, because I made them feel good, because I was their voice of reason, and because I was their collateral in a sense. In hindsight, I allowed myself to fulfill the personal desires of others and did not think about myself, even though I wanted a commitment. By the time I mentioned a relationship, it was too late. I got involved first and asked questions later. I did it all backwards, but I learned from it. I also ignored the obvious. I am comfortable enough to admit that.

I took "not right now or I am not ready" for when he is ready, he will choose me. But, as women (the young and the matured), we have to believe a man when he says that he is not ready, even if he is withholding that he wants to be with someone else. We have to love ourselves enough to be able to let go when relationships do not serve us. Rejection will have us holding on for dear life to a rope that we know cannot hold our weight. Letting go hurts but holding on is more damaging. We cannot afford to place ourselves on hold until he is ready -because he may never be ready (for us). And let's face it, we are too dope to be the back-burner bae! That is where the process of loving yourself comes in. It is a necessary process that takes knowing and loving God because He is the epitome of love, acknowledging that He loves you back, and He sees you greater than who you are in your current state. It takes strength, prayer, patience, work, accountability, and the ability to let go.

Please know that it is okay to be single. Use your single season(s) to get to know yourself. Use it to commune with the Father. Use it to learn, grow, and develop. Use it to start your business. Use it to evolve. Do not worry about a relationship. It will come. Do not focus your mind on when you will be in love again. It is okay to think about it, that is normal. However, we must not idolize relationships. Take the time to heal. When you have God, He loves you like no other. His word can literally serenade you to love Him into a place of contentment. His word shows His love for you because of His actions toward you. He will show you what love looks like by the way that He loves you. He will comfort you. He will cover you. He will send people to love you with His love. He will affirm you. He does this despite your love for Him. That is the unconditional, agape love of God. THIS has allowed me to love Him, which made me love myself differently, and love others (in spite of what I felt they deserved).

The more I desired to love God and love like He loved, the more I became free. How I saw myself was different. I learned to have an appreciation for myself that came by way of God's love. Loving myself more meant choosing me. It meant not accepting the same things that I accepted in the past. It literally woke me from a dead place with a renewed mind and turned my life around. God rescued me from myself.

I finally learned how to love others from a place of having a true love for myself. I had always loved others, but it was from a warped place because I did not love me; a place where I accepted toxic behaviors in the name of love. Not today. Loving me, means not settling or accepting toxicity. Loving you, means not allowing you to stay in my space to be toxic and being able to tell you that. It means that I will not hate you or hold a grudge because things didn't work out. It also means that forgiving you does not always equate to granting your access to becoming friends again.

What does your attitude toward other people say about you? A lack of love for yourself generally shows up in the friendships and relationships you pursue. Also, how you love yourself will show in the relationships that you remain in or flee.

Love moves people to kindness. Love is unselfish. It embraces everyone with gentleness, and not a harsh disposition. When you love correctly, people will experience the

God in you. My prayer has been for people to experience God when they come in contact with me. Essentially, who I am becoming and even what others have expressed about being around me has given the confirmation I need to know that I am on the right track, and I say that with a humble heart. When this happens, pay attention to what people say, because God is speaking. He has heard your prayers asking Him to show you who you are. Are you listening?

I AM NOT AFRAID TO SAY NO!

3

I never knew how much the word 'no' could be so liberating, especially when it came to dating. Listen, a man could be finer than Idris Elba (and that is hard to do), and I will tell him NO, now! Years ago...not so much. I would date and not have a purpose in mind. I loved food, and I loved not having to pay even more. Some dates would end in good night -and some would end *with* a good night. My excuse was: I am grown and single. I am just trying to have fun. But I did not realize how much lust was attached to my decisions and for my rationalization of being "grown."

Now let me put out a disclaimer, when I was 'dating' someone, it was just me and him. I was not sexing everybody that I hung out with or dated. However, I dated a lot because I had no idea what I was looking for. I literally had no plan. I was just going with the flow. I was also hurting and looking for love in all the wrong places. Even when the wrong place could not provide the love that I was searching for, I stayed because it felt like a safe place. Oh, was I deceived!

I created unhealthy soul ties or emotional attachments that were hard to sever. Soul ties are not always toxic. You can very well have a healthy soul tie with a person, especially in friendships. It becomes infiltrated and complicated usually with the opposite sex when intercourse is introduced, and then attempting to cut it off. Sex is what connects people. It is also spiritual and was made for marriage: Now concerning the matters about which you wrote: "It is good for a man not to have sexual relations with a woman." But because of the temptation to sexual immorality, each man should have his own wife and each woman her own husband (1 Corinthians 7:1-2 ESV). The Bible not only tells us that in marriage, the two become one flesh (Matthew 19:6), but he who is joined with a prostitute becomes one body with her (1 Corinthians 6:16 WEB). So, what do you think happens when YOU join with another person? You become one with them.

A soul tie is not a biblical term but is derived from the idea that people become connected through emotions and sex. And when a woman allows a man to enter her, she becomes a receiver of what he has in him. That is why it may be difficult to separate. Sex attaches people whether we would like to admit it or not.

Women become emotionally invested and so do men.

I did not know when I was younger, but now I understand why sex was meant for the marriage bed. It was never meant for us to become one with multiple people. When we do, we end up in situations that are hard to leave, especially when our identity and self-esteem are not intact. We stay in painful, dry places too long.

I already know what you are going to say, people get divorced and still end up with another person, right? Yes, we all know this to be true. But guess what? God HATES divorce (Malachi 2:16 KJV). A divorce is a tearing away or ripping away of two people; and when that happens, those people are left in bad shape. It does something to their spirits. So many people have been affected by divorce whether they wanted one or not. At some point in the process, they were hurt like hell, whether it was from discovery of infidelity or simply not wanting the divorce. People have to intentionally heal from it with blood, sweat, tears, and fears, I did it! (But I will talk about that in another book).

Present day, I choose to be abstinent. When I tell you that I never thought I could live without sex, I NEVER THOUGHT I COULD LIVE WITHOUT SEX! I never thought I could go days...weeks...months...or years. God is truly a deliverer. My decision to abstain had a lot to do with my evolving as a woman of God. In my twenties, I loved God and I even joined church on my own, but I was still living a little reckless and fornicating often, even in my thirties. I knew that God was a forgiving God, and I took that for granted. I was still getting myself into situations that were difficult to get out because of the emotional attachments. I knew that I had to make a choice though; either I could walk in obedience to the Father's voice or keep walking into revolving doors and getting deeply hurt. I chose obedience. It felt better. Pain relieved.

I could remember dealing with someone for years, but we never made it official. He said he was not ready, yet I was still involved with him as if he would change his mind. I was actually hoping he would. He did eventually, but it was after many years (10 off and on to be exact), and after much damage had been done. It was more of a rebound situation for the both of us. Shortly thereafter, I realized the true meaning of "the more things change, the more they stay the same." I obliged to an official relationship, but soon discovered that he was still doing what he was doing when we first met. He was lustful and had an insatiable appetite for women. I got tired of feeling like I was always competing for his heart and waiting for him to choose me. Why was I waiting? Sex was a blinder. I was pretty sure that I would never be his one and only. Somehow, I felt that I was winning, and he was the prize, not knowing that all along I was losing in my wait and that I was a prize the entire time! That situation lasted a New York minute. There had been several times that I said I would leave him alone, but this time it was different. I would let go never to return again. It was my final straw and set precedence for my decision-making for relationships to come. I was sick and tired of being sick and tired.

Never again will I settle for the "I am not ready" guy, the "I have been busy" guy, the "I do not know what I want" guy, the "let's just have fun" guy, or the "I am keeping my options open" guy. My answer to all of them is a hard NO because if they do not know where they are going, how can they lead me? So yeah...NO! I used to be blind, but I am delivert!

The 'I am not ready' guy may very well not be ready for a relationship, and that is okay. You never want to force a person to be with you. You cannot love a man into readiness, you cannot buy a man into readiness, and you cannot sex a man into readiness. If he is not ready and does not desire a relationship at all, move on if you desire one. But if you choose to date him anyway, do it without sex, please! Nonetheless, he could truly not be ready, or he could have decided that you are not the one he wants and does not want to tell you. You must be okay with both. And just because he does not want you does not mean that you are no longer worthy. Your worth is found in God. You were valuable before you met him and valuable shall you exit.

The 'I have been busy' guy is one who legit may be busy, but in his down time he does not reach out to you, he may not answer your calls or texts until several days later, but in the interim has time for everything else outside of you, including social media. Speaking of which, I remember a time when social media was not even a factor in dating and relationships. It has become a nuisance for some people.

Recently, I had the busy guy try to date me and talk sweet nothings whenever I was in his presence. He was quite the charmer. Our chemistry was amazing, and we actually went on several amazing dates. But I was not one of his priorities. A man is never too busy for the woman that he wants. And may I add, I have no problem with a man who is busy with work, his own business or life in general. BUT there has to be a point at some time in his day that he thinks about the woman he is trying to court and reaches out to her...especially if she has reached out to him. Guess what? He will if you are the one that he is into. I know what that feels like. The one who is genuinely interested will check up on you and make time, period. So, I said NO to that too. I appreciated the dates and the great conversations, but I am not okay with words (and apologies) without corrective action in motion. Show me and let me know it's real.

The 'I do not know what I want guy' at my age (almost 40), is way too seasoned to not know what he wants. And he also does not get to figure it out while he is with me. I cannot date someone who is unsure. More than likely, if he does not know what he wants or does not even have an idea, he could possibly be struggling with who he is. He could still be trying to heal from and even still brooding in his past relationships. I truly believe that when we know who we are, it is easier to identify what we want in others. We also get a clearer picture when we are in a healed place.

When I started dating in my young adult years, the number one question asked of me was, "What are you looking for in a man?" I would always say, I can tell you what I do not want. I would run down this semi-long list of pet peeves. One day, one of my best male friends challenged me. He asked, do you know who you are? I was literally stuck. It took me a while to answer his question. I had to dig deep. His question pushed me to think beyond who I was on the surface. That is when my "aha moment" came. I realized that I could not express what I was looking for because I did not know who I was.

It was not until I could identify who I was, that I was able to articulate what I wanted; and that meant what I wanted for life in general. I finally understood that when you know who you are, or have a pretty good idea, it is easier to gauge what you want, to make better decisions, and to have a vision regarding who you would like to become. It allows you to embrace your truth about the real you on the inside. Knowing who you are and standing in your truth can change your life tremendously. And this is why I do not have time for the one who says, he does not know what he wants. NO.

The 'let's just have fun' guy needs no explanation. He wants to be the fun guy and he wants you to be his fun girl. We all know what "fun" includes, right? Another NO for me, fam.

The 'I am keeping my options open' guy wants to keep a palate of women, just in case. Most times, that comes with a desire for various sexual relationships. If that is what you want, have at it. But I do not advise it. Some people feel that they have to date multiple people to find that one, and that is okay. Hell, you may even feel that way. I am not knocking you for what you desire. But if you have to sex 10 people to find 1...I dunno about that one. As far as Antonia goes, it's a NO. There may very well be a list of women that he is considering, but there are also men who know exactly what they want, and they pursue that. They pursue her. And I respect that.

I AM MUCH HAPPIER BECAUSE I REALIZED THAT A RELATIONSHIP DID NOT COMPLETE OR FULFILL ME!

4

One of the most cliche statements that I have heard people say is "my significant other completes me." And while it may feel that way, God does not send anyone to complete us because we are already whole people. He sends our complement. I know, semantics, right? Not really. Imagine a person who you thought completed you, leaving. Are you now incomplete or are you still a whole person who is now experiencing brokenness that can be healed? You do not have to add a new person to the mix to become complete, however, healing will restore you.

Our words have power. Death and life are in the power of the tongue, and those who love it will eat its fruit (Proverbs 18:21 NIV). If you believe they complete you, you will also feel like you cannot go on without them. Change what you say. Happiness, better yet, joy came from my healing and being okay with the fact that I can do things alone even if I did not want to.

When I was 14 years old, my dad gave me some money. I was home alone that weekend, so I asked him to drop me off at the movie theater. He asked, who are you going with? I replied, I am going alone because I am bored. That was the first time that I had never been to a movie unaccompanied. It made me realize that I could literally enjoy my own company.

Now, I enjoy doing those things with my own children. But I also take time out to treat myself. And in this season of waiting, I will not settle or tire of being able to have time to myself. Once I am married again, I know I will have to take my husband into consideration. No problem. So, if you are single like me, you better enjoy this time. Not saying that you cannot be an individual in marriage because you definitely can, but all of the things you enjoyed doing alone, you should now consider your significant other. Still, make sure you pamper yourself, and even if you need to get away to do something alone, do it. Just be considerate and communicate that. Communication is the bag.

Being both single and married has its advantages. Just know that your happiness should not be contingent on whether or not you are in a relationship. Keep evolving, keep improving, keep learning, keep going. The person that God has in mind for you will reap off of what you are experiencing and doing right now, and you will from what they are. Wherever you are has purpose, and when you two come together, you will be unstoppable. Enjoy this journey to your future, your promised future: For I know the plans I have for you, declares the Lord, plans to prosper you and not harm you, plans to give you hope and a future, (Jeremiah 29:11 NIV).

I AM ASKING THE IMPORTANT QUESTIONS IN THE BEGINNING!

5

I am no longer afraid of asking the important questions in the beginning and being afraid that it would run a man off. If he flees, he flees! He was not for me. Due to insecurities within, I used to be afraid of the answers or even that my question would make a man run. I no longer deal with that insecurity nor am I afraid of rejection, so I am going to ask what I need to know...in the beginning! I do not want to waste my time or have you to waste yours. See how considerate I am?

I remember being frightened of asking a man about his intentions with me. I was more afraid of his answer more than anything. What if he said he did not want me? That he did not want a relationship? So, I did not ask. I just went with the flow. I thought, eventually he will like me more as we continue to talk. Besides, I am the cool, down to earth woman that everyone likes, right? Yes, people liked me, but they wanted to have multiple flavors of cake; and they ate all of the cakes. Again, there was nothing wrong with me, but I took that as rejection.

Even though some people may lie, I still need to know what I need to know up front. His actions will soon reveal the truth. This cuts to the chase so that I do not waste too much time. If I ask a man about what his intentions are and he cannot tell me, then the one thing he can count on is being counted out. You cannot show up to a job interview ill prepared and expect to get the job. It is my duty to myself to vet my potential mate as it is his to find out the same things about me. No longer are the days that I do not ask questions first, find myself in a situationship, then ask questions later. No one should do that.

If a man is expressing interest in me, I want to know what he is looking for. Most times, men will tell you the truth. If he is not looking for anything serious, and just wants to take you out on dates as friends, he is probably going to tell you that. And there is absolutely nothing wrong with that. If he just wants to "have a good time" he is probably going to tell you that. If he wants a relationship and not marriage, he is probably going to tell you that too. If he desires marriage with someone, he is definitely going to tell you that. How you proceed, depends on what you are looking for and what you want. I don't mind hanging out as platonic friends. However, as I explained earlier, a man who expresses that he is looking for a good time (sex) is not an option for me. If I continued, that would almost be like giving the green light to "go there" with me because he told me the truth and I stayed around. I would not feel the need to go on unnecessary dates with him or waste more money and time...unless he is buying tacos! I am kidding. That is an inside joke between me and one of my close friends, DB!

Nonetheless, it is important to vet the person who you are dating. Whether they want children or not, is an important question to ask. Essentially, there are many questions that need to be asked, but get the pertinent ones out of the way, especially the ones that could possibly be deal breakers. What are your deal breakers? Ask those questions.

Asking a man about his beliefs is critical to me. I desire a man who loves God and that I can trust to lead me and our family. And because I believe in the word of God, it gives us specific instructions for relationships, not just romantic ones. I use it as a guide for what I want in my life; to understand what I have and need in my life. God will never steer us wrong, so if we listen to Him, even the small still voices that He speaks, we will begin to hear them more audibly and clearly. We just have to be willing to listen. And many times, I even failed at that. I always tried to justify a man's actions or make excuses for him when all along God was like, daughter what are you doing?! You asked me to show you, I showed you and now you do not believe me. And when that happens, you have to go through the fire and unfortunately get burned. Obedience is golden.

WHEN SOMEONE SHOWS YOU WHO THEY ARE, BELIEVE THEM!

(MAYA ANGELOU)

STOP giving chance after chance for someone to keep disappointing you. I super love this quote from Maya Angelou. And though it wreaks of common sense, we all know that common sense is not all that common amongst the people. It sometimes takes us a while to get "it." It takes getting to know a person to see what kind of person they really are, but it does not take long to find out. That is when you are shown who they are. And you better believe what you see! How are they with other people? How do they treat the wait staff? How do they treat you? Are they liars? Are they cheaters? Do they have children? How do they treat their children? What is their relationship with the other parent?

It would behoove you to ignore what you see. I have noticed that some people make too many excuses, especially after seeing for themselves. Let me rephrase that, because you have to be accountable for yourself. "I" have made too many excuses in the past. I always wanted to believe that there was a greater good in people; that they did not mean to treat me badly because they may be going through something. And I did this even after asking God to show me if they were for me or not. Here is a word of advice: When you pray and ask God to show you something, believe what you see and listen to what you hear. If you do it your way, it typically leads to detriment.

I even had excuses when I knew that I heard from the Lord. I would then second guess and say, maybe it is me. Maybe I am tripping. Maybe my standards are too high. I even had 'friends' tell me that I was too picky. But now I know that God was literally molding me and molding my desires and expectations for who He had chosen for me: Delight yourself in the LORD, and he will give you the desires of your heart (Psalm 37:4 NIV). He placed better desires on the inside of me. I was not trippin!

I was tired of getting my feelings hurt, but I could not blame anyone else because I made my own decisions and I had to suffer the consequences. Ignoring the obvious will lead you into a pit. Listen, with your eyes and your ears. Believe what they are telling you. Do not make excuses for them. You deserve someone who shows you love and shows you goodness. You deserve a person of good character. You deserve someone who will acknowledge and not ignore you. You deserve a person who does not mind speaking your love language. And if you are a believer, you deserve the person who God has for you. He absolutely has someone specifically for you, and you will meet them when it is time. You may have already met. You may have dated in the past. I do believe that you could have dated the right person, but at the wrong time.

One thing that I cannot stress enough is to stop giving people chance after chance to disappoint you. Have you ever heard the saying, 'Fool me once, shame on you? Fool me twice, shame on me?" Sooo...how many times do you need to be fooled? How many chances are you going to give? How long are you going to suffer and die on the inside because you are trying to see the best in people? How much longer will it be until you realize that you are not their personal Savior? Why are you addicted to pain? There is something that drives you to be the way you are. Pray and find out what it is. Look at your family dynamic. How were you raised? What have you been through? You will find an answer. And when you do, pray for deliverance. Pray for healing. Pray for freedom! Get some help.

I know we give chances because deep down we believe that they can change, or because we have too much time invested. And let's be honest, we do not want to start over with someone else, so we fight and fight until there is nothing left. I literally just had a vision of a skeleton as I was writing this, and what I got from that is every time this happens, a piece of us deteriorates. We become as lifeless as a skeleton because our focus has now become immersed with this person that we are not gaining from, yet they are subtracting. We are allowing for spiritual and mental bankruptcy because we are not listening to God and still hoping for man. But thanks to the Father, He restores us back to good health and a full life.

IF I WANT SOMETHING SERIOUS, I CANNOT SETTLE FOR "THIS" UNTIL "THAT" COMES ALONG.

7

One of the most important lessons that I have learned is that I can function greatly without a romantic relationship and without sex. Whew chile...what a lesson! I always knew that I would be okay when not in a relationship, but I did not always think that I could be abstinent; even as a church going, faith-filled woman. If I wanted sex back then, I could get it. But it costs too much. It cost me my emotions, my mind, my body, and gave me soul ties. It costs too much! Have I fallen since my decision to become abstinent 4 years ago?

Yes. And it cost me, which is why I have chosen to be kept. Legs closed. Lock the door, but don't throw away the keys...I need them for later.

When it comes to settling for this until that comes along, there are people who have seat fillers in place in the event that another person does not work out. I am not a seat filler. There are those who feel they cannot function without some kind of romantic relationship with the opposite sex. I am not that person either. In the past though, I thought that was the way it was supposed to be done. I am not knocking anyone who is where I was in my past because I know the struggle. I just want to help you. It was hard to get out of that life without God. The pain that was attached was my motivator to get out. I just want you to reevaluate your situation. Are you truly happy or are you dying a little on the inside because you are settling? Why are you settling? You were meant to have God's best for your life. When I realized that, my life changed.

But before that, all I knew was that I wanted someone to fill the empty space until I met someone else. The caveat was that it was not easy because I was still attached emotionally, which is not fair to the next person. I thought I could detach. I tried. My way of trying to detach or prove that nothing was there was to be mean. I would not answer my phone, and essentially ghost someone until I found out if the new thing would work out. Yep, I did that. And if you are reading this. I apologize. I was lost.

For a long time, I wondered why things did not work out for me, but I had no blueprint or guidance on how to date. I did what I perceived was the right thing to do. And I was doing it wrong. There were times that I had wished that I could have learned at an early age about being a kept woman, but that is not my story. Besides, I went through what I went through so that I could write this! And our stories are powerful. We are overcome by the blood of the lamb and the power of our testimony (Revelation 12:11 NIV). I encourage you to tell your story so that you could help others too. There are people you do not know who are depending on your story. They do not know it and neither do you. One of my favorite women to listen to is Iyanla Vanzant, and one of my favorite quotes from her is, "whenever you stand and tell your story, not only do you heal yourself but you heal others."

As I write about how I settled for this, until that came along, it has helped me to realize my truth. I hurt and used some people in the process because I wanted them around for my personal reasons. And then I dropped them. Not only did I hurt others, I was hurting myself. I was ignorant of what was going on in my life, but now I see. And as wisdom and understanding would have it, I have learned from my mistakes and I am a better person because of it.

At this point in my life, I do not desire to date anyone just to say I am dating. I refuse to play with a person's emotions or have anyone play with mine. I do not have the desire to obtain a "boy toy" to hold me off until "Mr. Right" comes along. Instead of settling for this, until that comes along, I desire to wait. And while I wait, I will continue to focus and work on my goals and dreams.

HEALING IS IMPORTANT...FOR YOU AND FOR THEM.

8

Let them go through their process. Do not sell yourself short trying to fix someone who is broken. You can encourage them, you can even pray for them, but you are not their savior! I cannot emphasize that enough. Before entering a relationship, make sure the person is healed in some capacity. This is imperative because most people who are unhealed end up becoming toxic in relationships, and not just romantic ones. I do not believe their being toxic is intentional, but it comes with the territory of having unchecked and unresolved issues. How do you know if a person is healed or not? Pay close attention to their conversation. You can tell a lot about a person by simply listening to their thoughts and observing their actions. However, if you move too fast, you cannot gauge the relationship with sober eyes. Lust has made you drunk. And drunkenness impairs judgment.

One of the tell-tale signs is that they live in the past. All of their conversations end up diverting to something that happened with their ex(es), so much so that they are oblivious to it. I remember dating a guy, and we began to discuss things we would like to do and places that we would like to go. Before I knew it, he cut me off and ran down a list of places he and his ex used to go, what they did, and how he missed those things. He even sent me pictures of her and her children to show me "how it used to be" when he was a family man. He replayed this story one too many times. Clearly, brother man was not over his ex. Major turnoff and major red flag. You probably know where that went, right? Nowhere.

Even as I can recall what he did, I also recollect doing the same. However, I knew I was not over my ex. I tried to move on without healing first. I thought having another person would help me get over him. It did not. I had to take it upon myself to be honest and say that I was not ready.

When two unhealed people come together who live in their past, it could be a recipe for disaster. In these situations, there will be two people who are never satisfied, two people who are unhappy, two people who are frustrated with one another and seek outside attention, two people who do not trust one another, two people who are confused, and the list goes on. You could very well carry what happened in your last relationship into your new one. Give yourself time.

It is important to make sure that you are healed to some degree because I do believe that some things may show up later. It may show up in your next relationship. And sometimes, you may be able to walk that out with that person. But please make sure you partner with God in your healing process first. And most importantly, make sure the person you are dating has gone through their process as well.

LISTEN TO WHAT HE SAYS (AND DOES NOT SAY) BUT OBSERVE WHAT HE DOES!

9

We all know, or should know that actions speak much louder than words, right? I cannot count how many times I have made the mistake of not observing the actions of people and solely being dependent on the words that proceeded from their mouths. I always assumed that because I was intentional about being a person of my word, that other people would be too. That is not always the case.

I dated a guy who I felt was a true romantic. He always spoke words of affirmation toward me and expressed how excited he was to date me each time we went out. He was chivalrous and a great conversationalist, which was right up my alley. He prayed before we ate, and he blushed when I would gaze at him. It was cute. We had known each other for over 20 years. I was digging him. But, his actions…(insert the hand over the face emoji)! In between the times that we would hang out, there would be minimal conversation between the two of us. There had been a few times that we had gone 3 weeks or longer without talking. I was not bothered at first because I was pleased with the pace that we were going. However, I was bothered by the fact that he did not call, especially after missing a call from me. I expressed my feelings about his non communication which had become habitual. He apologized and said that he would work on it. The problem was, after being missing in action, he offered to take me on dates so that he could explain. But, the 'let me explain' dates became old, so I bowed out.

When someone is interested, there will be some sort of pursuit. A man who is interested in a woman is going to come for her. He is going to call or even text her because she ran across his mind at some point in the day. And he is going to return her calls if he has missed them. There is nothing deep or prolific about this. It is literally common sense.

Listening to what someone says and does not say and observing what they do will save you from heartbreak. It will also keep you from wasting too much of your valuable time. You cannot fill in their blanks for what you want them to mean. And please do not assume anything. Ask questions if you are unclear about a thing. But even when a person is not answering, they are indeed answering. Listen and take heed. Be an observer for your own sake.

There is beauty in being able to recognize and discern when a person is not good for you. That is God's protection. There is more beauty in not being mad at the fact that they are not for you and having the ability to keep it moving gracefully. That's emotional intelligence. You have to learn to see past the things that check off your list. Yes, he is romantic, but does he call you? Yes, he is ambitious, but does he make excuses for seeing you? You deserve someone who is romantic AND calls you; someone who is ambitious AND makes it a point to see you. You can have both.

IF YOU BELIEVE IN GOD, AND YOU HEAR FROM HIM, DO NOT SECOND GUESS IT!

10

How many times can you count that you have not listened to God; that when you prayed and asked God to give you a sign (specifically relational), He gives you one? Not only that, you question yourself and start to make excuses for what you saw (your own understanding)? Never underestimate God's voice.

Trust in the Lord with all your heart; do not depend on your own understanding. Seek His will in all you do, and He will show you which path to take (Proverbs 3:5-6 NLT).

You cannot afford to make justification for other people's behaviors, especially when He reveals who they are or that they are not a good fit for you. Sometimes, His giving you revelation or confirmation is not an indication that the person is bad, but the person is not right for you at that time. You may not be right for them. Or could it be that you are not as ready as you think? Right person, wrong time? What if God is still preparing and refining you? Whatever it is, trust God. If you seek His will, He will give you direction. Do not be surprised if He reveals YOU to you. Yes, I said that.

By this time, you should feel as though we are besties because I have shared a lot about my "love life" with you...so here we grow again. I have asked God more times than I can count to give me signs about guys that I have dated or would potentially date, that I eventually stopped asking. Why? There was ALWAYS something; something that was literally a deal breaker for me. The disappointments were rather discouraging and painful. Unfortunately, in those times, I did not perceive it as God's protection or answered prayers. All I knew was that I wanted what I wanted because I had the free will to choose; so, I shut God out. Obviously, I cannot be trusted with myself.

Shutting God out, allows the enemy to come in. Isolation from God is unsafe. In this place, deception and trickery is inevitable. I cannot say it enough to include God. You should not hear from Him and then hide. Every single thing you do, everywhere you go, take God with you because it could be a matter of life and death. Have you ever tried things on your own and they simply did not work out? When you allow God to step in, He will show you why.

THERAPEUTIC HELP DOES NOT MAKE YOU CRAZY, IT HELPS YOU GAIN CLARITY

11

In the Black community, the subject of counseling is gaining momentum, but there has always been a stigma associated with going to counseling or therapy. Growing up, I heard so many people say that counseling was for crazy people, that I was reluctant to go when I needed to as an adult. Before you ask, yes, I do believe that God is a healer. I also believe that He made counselors and therapists to assist with our mental health, just as He created us for our purpose here on the Earth. God uses people. Listen, sometimes we just have to sit down on somebody's couch. It aids in our healing process.

I sought out a therapist about 4 years ago. I was having such a hard time when I was going through divorce. I experienced so many emotions at once, that I knew it was time to get help. I will not elaborate much about that part of my life. You will read about that later. I sought wise counsel from my pastor's wife who eventually became a good friend. She was instrumental in helping me through my process. And eventually, I hired a therapist.

I still remember the first session with my therapist. I could not stop crying, but it felt good for me to dump all of that on him, poor guy. I do not remember all of the questions he asked, but they forced me to think deeply and caused me to weep. My sessions had gone from my pointing toward the ex-husband, to looking within and searching for my significance. I was significant before I was married, significant during marriage, and I am significant now. I am essential (wink).

He had me read the book, The Search for Significance by Robert S. McGee. This book forced me to journey through my thoughts and deal with my emotions. The questions allowed me to see how much rejection played a part in my life and how it affected me, the people pleasing behaviors I had, the lies that I believed from the enemy, and pointed me toward God's love and acceptance. I was faced with truths about myself that were hard to accept, but critical to start my process.

Before each session, we would discuss what I read. He became impressed with how I was starting to progress. I started having the ability to answer questions without wailing. I started to become okay and have peace with the fact that my marriage may or may not work. Only God could have done something like that. I was still hurting, but I had to stand face to face with it. I was handling my pain a lot better. It helped me gain clarity on who I was independently, as well as who we were as a couple. But I still had a long way to go.

Attending therapy made me realize that way more people should obtain therapy, not because there is something wrong with them per se, but to gain clarity about their own lives. I knew many people who were hurting. People who believed in God, and people who did not. People who just wanted to figure out how to get better. And it is my belief that God makes us better, and yet He still allows people like counselors and therapists to help us get to the root of our problems. So here is my advice to you: go to therapy.

ANGER IS A DETERRENT TO HEALTHY COMMUNICATION!

12

I am a huge fan of revisiting a conversation when you are no longer angry: A gentle answer turns away wrath, but a harsh word stirs up anger (Proverbs 15:1 KJV). As I have grown older and much more mature, I realized how wise it was to sometimes just keep quiet or simply calm down so that I could understand what the other party was communicating. It does not mean that I am backing down, but it means that I am choosing wisdom because I know it could go one of two ways. How you react determines the direction of the dialogue. Plus, I have learned to relish in peace. It feels much better.

Black women have gotten a bad rep for being vocal, and I will not back down from being vocal if the situation calls, however, I will use wisdom in my delivery. I know because I have been tried, tested, and proven on several occasions. I have literally had to become intentional about not responding in a negative way. There is not a single person over the last 4 years (since I chose peace as my priority) who can tell you that I am an angry or bitter person, or that I have had an argument with them.

Why did I say that anger is a deterrent to healthy communication? Most times during an argument, either one or both parties are not listening because they are trying to defend themselves and get their points across. It takes the mature to listen and then reply. Anger adds fuel to the fire and nothing healthy can come from a mouth full of flames. It tears down, damaging everything in its path. I know because I used to shoot fiery darts with my tongue and did not apologize for it. This is no way to live. Having anger or any form of bitterness in your heart, makes you feel worse. It takes away from your internal joy and it takes away from your peace. It is okay to be angry. The word even tells us:

Be ye angry, and sin not: let not the sun go down upon your wrath: Neither give place to the devil (Ephesians 4:26-27 KJV).

Having said that, we need to find out what healthy communication looks like. And although it may feel uncomfortable, it is something we must practice. It involves listening, which is the most important aspect of healthy communication, being honest and transparent, and getting out of your feelings by using your emotional intelligence.

No one wants to communicate with someone who does not listen. We must humble ourselves and allow people to speak and be mature enough to reply after considering what the other person has expressed. And when we are able to do that, we can have healthy, 2-way communication. It is effective when both people can walk away with an understanding of the issue. But we must learn to attack the issue and not each other.

THEY CANNOT LOVE YOU CORRECTLY IF THEY DO NOT LOVE THEMSELVES

13

Have you ever heard an older person say, "be with the one who loves you more than they love themselves?" No disrespect to the older generation, but I do not agree with that statement. I would much rather be with a man who loves himself, not only that, a man who loves God. God is the essence of love and we can learn a lot from how He loves us.

Let's just talk about His love for a moment! For God SO loved the world, that he GAVE (John 3:16 KJV). I could have typed out the rest of the scripture, but I wanted to focus on what love does. Love GIVES. Love is an action. We did not have to do anything for God's love, and He displayed an action toward us even when we did not deserve it. Not only did He love us, He SO loved us. Let me show you the power of "so." Someone could say, thank you for the flowers or thank you SO much for the flowers. They could say, I love you or I love you SO much! "SO" shows an added level of appreciation. It describes the excess of the verb that comes before it.

I stated in a previous chapter that how you love yourself usually reflects in the people you choose to love. When you lose your sense of value, you are more apt to choose relationships that are unhealthy because of the need to fill some void. You blame love for the reason you stay, however, not knowing your worth coupled with having a soul tie will trick your heart into believing that it is love. That ain't love! That is a need for healing, deliverance, and restoration. What you think you are missing cannot be found in, on top of, or under another person. I pray that you begin to have a sense of what real love is and realize how significant you really are, especially in God's eyes.

When a person does not love themselves, it is impossible to love others correctly. They can try, but how much more do you think a person could love you when they truly love themselves: Love the Lord your God with all your heart and with all your soul and with all your mind and with all your strength. The second is this: Love your neighbor as yourself. There is no commandment greater than these (Mark 12:30-31 KJV). Your neighbor is anyone who is next to you. The word tells us to love our neighbors as we love ourselves, and my question remains, how can a person love you if they do not love themselves? They can only love from the measure of love that they have available. Will that be enough for you?

BUILD PURPOSEFUL RELATIONSHIPS!

One of my most consistent prayers is asking that God connects me to those who are suitable for my destiny. That does not always mean that things will be good, but whatever happens is needed for my growth. Purposeful relationships are so critical that it essentially determines where you go. If you have people around you who have no desire to go higher, you may become stagnated because essentially, you are only as strong as the weakest person on your team. Eventually, you will reach a plateau, but you must break through and move upward if that is your desire. If you can influence them to go up, go up!

God wants us to have purposeful relationships and even warns us about being out of purpose with them: Do not be misled: Bad company corrupts good character (1 Corinthians 15:33 KJV). Be mindful of the company you keep. Try to be intentional about discerning people's places in your life. There may even be people that you are in relationship with who have no desire for movement or what I would like to call, anchored. And they may be comfortable there. What happens in comfortability? Nothing grows. What happens when you anchor a boat? The boat stays in one place until the anchor is pulled to go to the next destination. If the people you are with are not willing to pull the anchor and continue to move forward, that is a clear indication that you must jump out if you do not want to remain stuck. Man overboard! And guess what? It will not kill you.

You need the same relational intelligence for the person you choose to date, specifically if you are one who is dating for a purpose. Would you purposely choose someone who has no desires, no goals, no aspirations? One of the best quotes that I have heard about relationships was, when a man wants you, he will have a destination (Pastor Jerry Flowers). Where are you going with this person? No... really...ask yourself, where are we going? If you cannot answer, or he is unsure, what is the purpose of your relationship?

Refer back to Chapter 5, asking the important questions in the beginning. Please ask the important questions, and that will tell you the forecast. Are you willing to go out to sea without knowing the weather? I hope you said, no.

DIVORCE PAST RELATIONSHIPS THAT ARE IN YOUR HEAD!

15

Nothing will disappoint you faster than expecting your ex(es) in someone else. Divorce that thought and focus on what you learned through your pain. Not only is it unfair to you, it is unfair to the other person because it does not provide them with a leveled playing ground. It keeps you from seeing a potential mate for who they truly are. It keeps you from having the opportunity of meeting good people and maintaining successful relationships. This type of thinking insinuates that you are not healed and that your expectations are unreasonable. There is nothing wrong with having preferences, but if you want *what* you used to have, then go back to *who* you used to have. Tell me how that works out for you. But if you want something new, something different, be open to accepting a person for what comes with them, and not your preconceived expectations without a discussion involving that person. Do not try and make them into what you want them to be.

Not only should we not try and change someone else, we must beware of a person who tries to change us. That is a form of control and that is a toxic behavior trait. If your "enough" is not good enough for them, you are with the wrong person. And if you change who you are for someone else, you will end up regretting your decision and resenting that person when your relationship does not work out (or does), or you see that you have not reached personal goals because you were focused on attaining goals to appease someone else.

I have conversed with women who have said they changed for a man. When he wanted a slim girl, she got lipo for him. When he wanted a girl who had long hair, she installed weave for him. When he wanted a woman with short hair, she cut all of her hair for him. When he wanted a woman who wore fashion labels, she went over her budget and maxed out credit cards for him. When he wanted a woman to wait on him -hand and foot, she was on all fours for him. When he wanted her to be with other women, she got turned out for him. But she did all of that in hopes of obtaining a ring that she never received. What happens then? She starts to beat herself up for changing and losing herself for someone who did not choose her. Her self-esteem becomes even more shot. She feels rejected. She is heartbroken because she did not know how to choose herself first. She did not know what it meant to love herself. She lost her identity. She only knew to give of herself because that made her feel wanted. And while she was giving, all they were doing was taking. She was depleted. Lost. Stuck. And she never sought-after God in her relationships.

I literally had someone tell me that he was conflicted because he was looking for me in his new relationship; that he had not healed from our relationship before he moved on. He expected her to do things that I had done down to the personality. He said that he regretted losing me and said it was one of the biggest regrets he had ever had. But as a person of integrity and a person who intentionally tries to do what is right, I told him that he had to divorce the idea of me from his head and give her a fair chance; that maybe if he gave up the idea of her being like me, that it would cause his eyes to become unclouded and that he would not judge her. Then, he could truly see her and love her correctly.

I am not a fan of taking revenge against others or clapping in the face of hurting people or those who I feel are reaping what they have sown. And he told me that...that he was reaping from what happened between the two of us. Nonetheless, who am I to say that what a person is going through is because of me? I am very careful of that and I do not take pride in rejoicing in anyone's pain or loss.

Fantasizing about your past or desiring your exes in others can write you a ticket that you cannot afford to pay. It can halt your progression and end your relationships. Focus on what is in front of you because you may very well miss something. If you find that hard to do,

I suggest that you seek therapy. There is a reason behind all of this, especially if you desire to change who you are to fit into someone's box.

LAST, BUT NOT LEAST

I pray that you find your true identity and that you begin to find peace with who God made you to be. When He made you, he made you perfect. Not perfect as in having no flaws, but perfect meaning complete. Because...well, you are enough!

Although my life has been a series of ups and downs, I am thankful for the fact that God kept me and carried me through it all; that my mental health stayed intact, and that I actually learned some valuable lessons. There will come a point in time when you will become sick and tired of being sick and tired, and that will be the push you need to make a change. You have to be intentional about your own well-being.

We have God, we have the Bible, we have pastors, we have self-help books, friends, and parents, but nothing will change if you do not decide to change. It is okay to focus on you. And with that, it is highly possible that you will lose relationships. You may realize that even those relationships may have been formed because the only thing you had in common was pain.

If you get nothing else from this book, I want you to know that you were always enough because that is how God made you. He made you a complete person and everything you need is already on the inside of you. You will pull from it when the time arises. He did not create you for other people to add value to you. You may have made unwise decisions like I did, but you can be redeemed. Life for you as you know it can be changing in the twinkling of an eye.

I want you to fight for yourself. Fight for you like you fight for your children and the rest of your family, your friends, injustice, and worthy causes...because you are a worthy cause. Your life matters.

If you have been struggling to get out of a situation, I want you to tell someone you trust who has the ability to help you walk away. It is still your decision, but having accountability will help you tremendously, especially if you are honest. It is time to stop with the excuses. When you know better, it is a must that you start to do better. Obedience goes a long way, and it will save your life.

Fasting helps. If you can control or have discipline over what you eat, then you will garner strength to say no in other areas of your life. You may also fall, as I have before, but do not keep falling on purpose. Fasting has helped me become more disciplined, so when it comes to sex, it is a no-brainer. I refuse to allow it to return me to the old me. I was not brought out to be defeated, but because I have the victory in Christ Jesus!

God allowed me to travel to my past to write this book, and honestly, I was reluctant. I was afraid that I would be judged. Then He said, daughter, there are many who have gone through situations and have been afraid to tell their stories. When you break your silence, others will break theirs. They will identify, people will be healed, and people will be moved to be transparent about their own issues of love and pain.

There are people that you do not know who will not be healed until you tell your story! Tell it! And remember, no matter what anyone tells you, you are enough! You were always enough.

I thank God for allowing me to share a part of my life with you. I cannot go back to who I used to be, because I now know who I am. I am a child of the most high God. From the beginning, I WAS ALWAYS ENOUGH!

Connect with Antonia on social media:

Facebook: @authorantonia

IG: @antoniabjohnson

WWW.ANTONIABJOHNSON.COM

www.ingramcontent.com/pod-product-compliance
Lightning Source LLC
Chambersburg PA
CBHW071905070526
44583CB00016B/1857